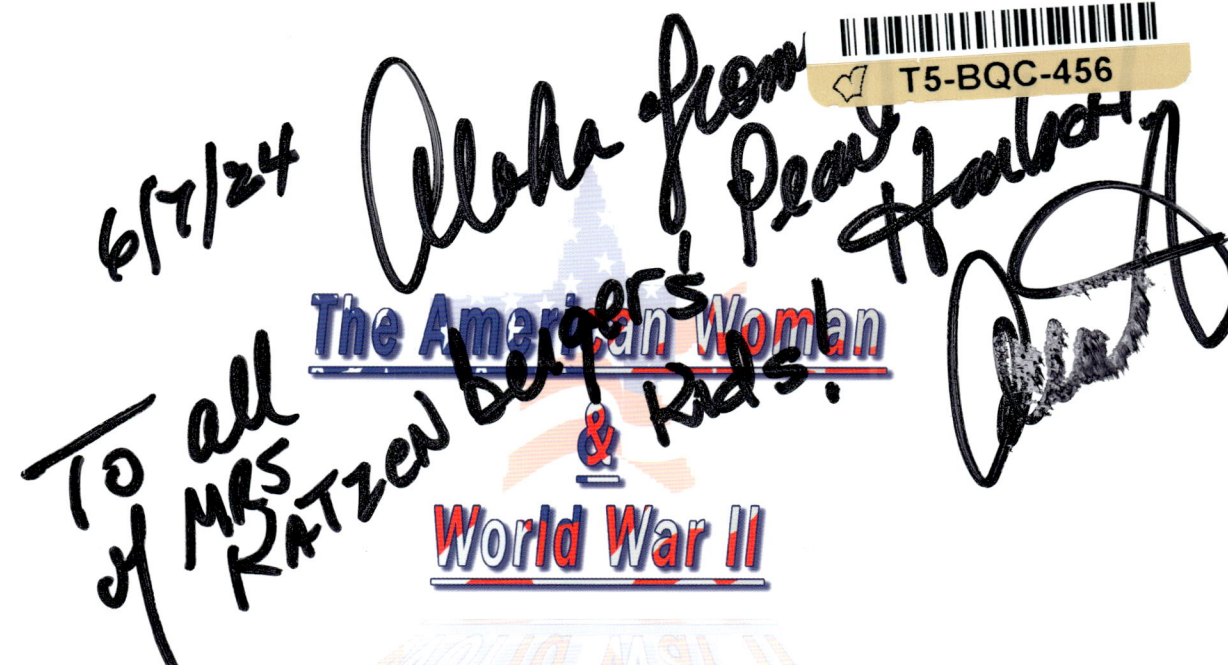

The American Woman & World War II

A HandHeld History

By Allan Seiden

A call to action drew America's women into World War II. It was a demanding and transformative experience, centuries in the making.

Nothing would have the emancipating impact on American women as did the six long years (1939-1945) of World War II. For women, as for men, the war was a transformational time, demanding sacrifice and communal effort rooted in patriotism and the very real sense that this was a battle for survival.

During the First World War women had played a supporting role, buying war bonds, nursing the wounded, serving as volunteers, and encouraging their husbands and sons with declarations of patriotism and pride. It fell to women to maintain

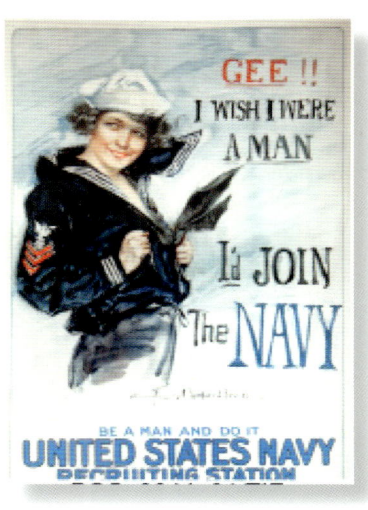

George Washington hands Betsy Ross a star for the flag she is sewing for the new nation, in a postcard c.1900. A Navy poster for World War I plays on the theme of the military as a man's domain.

It was the need for workers that changed things in ways that were largely unanticipated when women were recruited to take a hands-on role in pursuit of victory, both as civilians and in the Armed Forces.

the structure of family and home while the men fought on distant fronts. In terms of human history, it was a pattern repeated in most cultures, a reality rooted in our species primeval past.

Even in places and at times when women accompanied their men into war, as happened in more ancient, tribal times, they did not serve as combatants, although they might well have become the spoils of war for the victors after the men were killed. In Viking belief, winged females called Valkyrie accompanied men into battle, not to fight, but to escort those who were slain to the heavenly halls of Valhalla, where their courage was eternally rewarded. Likewise, stories of Amazons and other warrior women are more legend than fact, with women almost universally serving as nurturing caregivers.

There were many individual variations in just how that played out, but even as technology was transforming society, redefining man's relationship to nature and survival, it remained the traditional mind set in almost all cultures. In World War II, circumstances demanded an end to that rigid division of roles, which were already breaking down under the impact of enfranchisement, boom times, and the Great Depression.

It was the demand for "manpower" created by World War II that set things in motion, with the scale of the Second World War making a

Valkyrie, female beings of Viking legend, accompany warriors into battle, deciding who would be slain, then escorting them to a hero's afterlife in Valhalla.

crucial difference, providing a new meaning to the very concept of war.

World War I devastated Europe from 1914 through 1918, leaving behind destroyed villages and cities, with fatalities counted in the tens of millions. Ruefully called *"…the war to end all wars…"* for its catastrophic impact, within 20 years it would be far outdone in scale and death count, as ideology and geopolitical policies allied Nazi Germany, fascist Italy, and militarist Japan in an alliance focused on world domination.

Opposition to that objective would first draw in Great Britain, which declared war on Germany in September 1939, when Poland, its ally, was invaded and subjugated within days by the Nazi *blitzkrieg* ("lightening war"). Belgium, Holland, Denmark and France were likewise invaded and rapidly economically integrated into the Third Reich.

For two years, Britain, supplied by America, which was officially neutral, resisted the German juggernaut alone, victim of countless air raids and attacks at sea. In June 1940, a British armada evacuated 340,000 people from the French port of Dunkirk, including 140,000 members of the French Army who fought alongside the British under the independent command of General Charles de Gaulle. Initially, the Soviet Union remained on the sidelines thanks to a non-aggression pact signed by Hitler and Stalin in August 1939, paving the way for the German invasion of Poland and its

Thousands await evacuation from Dunkirk, France, June 1940.

dismemberment by Germany and the Soviet Union. Two years later Hitler betrayed Stalin, invading Russia and drawing the Soviets into an alliance with Great Britain that added a second European front to the war.

The United States was not drawn into the war until Dec. 8, 1941, following the Japanese attack on Pearl Harbor. Japan had already set out to establish itself as a world power, invading Manchuria in 1931 and establishing a puppet kingdom called Manchukuo. In 1937 Japan invaded China proper, brutally subjugating its people, while casting an eye on the resource-rich colonies of Dutch Indonesia, French Indochina, British Burma and India, and America's Philippine commonwealth.

The dominoes of war fell into place when Germany, fulfilling its treaty obligation to Japan, declared war on the United States on December 9, 1941. With battles raging across Europe, North Africa, and in Atlantic waters, across Asia and the far-flung archipelagoes of the Pacific, a truly worldwide war was now underway.

Pearl Harbor, Dec. 7, 1941, with Battleship Row ablaze.

At the same time, technological advances in weaponry and delivery systems had made mass murder a part of warfare, with the line between military and civilian casualties often disregarded. In scale and brutality, WWII dwarfed all prior wars.

Millions of European women and children were included in the war's grim statistics. American women were largely shielded from life-threatening violence by America's distance from the front lines, although the war stirred fears of attack from the sea by Germany in the Atlantic, and Japan in the Pacific. America's isolation made her the production hub of the Allied war effort.

Initially, there was some resistance to including women directly in the war effort. It was a prejudice the government fought against as the demands of war set changes in motion that would quickly redefine what might be expected of America's women.

A Vichy French poster plays on female vulnerability. Women and children are portrayed as victims of the depraved British, propaganda trumping the truth of Nazi brutality.

As far back as the mid-1860s, following the end of the Civil War, American Suffragettes had labored vigorously to secure the vote for American women. There was irony in the fact that newly freed male slaves, whose cause had been championed by women, were now enfranchised, but women were not.

It would prove a hard and long-fought battle, the way blocked by those who considered the franchise a male-only privilege of citizenship. That view was widespread. Prior to World War I, in fact, only Australia, New Zealand, and the Scandinavian countries had enfranchised women.

A Suffragette rally, c. 1900 (left). It took more than 50 years countering stiff opposition on many fronts (above) before the 19th Amendment, passed in 1920, secured a woman's right to vote. That outcome was supported by the many contributions of women toward the victory in WWI, which ended in 1918.

In 1920, however, just two years after the end of the First World War, the 19th Amendment was enacted into law, granting American women the right to vote. It was just the start of what would prove an on-going pursuit of gender equality, also redefining, in the process, the limits of personal freedom.

The Roaring Twenties, a decade-long era of boom times and social emancipation, saw high-kicking flappers and their partners dancing away the last vestiges of Victorian propriety. Times were wild, prohibition setting off a nationwide surge in violent criminal activity. Factories opened and cities rapidly grew, drawing immigrants from abroad and from America's rural heartland, which remained far more committed to a conservative outlook and traditional values.

America's "melting pot" cities offered women anonymity and a ballooning number of office jobs and careers that had not existed a generation earlier. New technologies paved the way to mass production and affordability for a consumer-fueled, super-charged economy. Away from home, new standards prevailed, and many women sought the freedom and excitement the Roaring Twenties offered as the decade raced toward a frantic finale.

Seemingly over night, prosperity was replaced by sobering times of mass unemployment, breadlines, and the social uncertainty that marked the '30s as a decade of diminished expectations and government intervention.

A flapper (left) symbol of the Roaring Twenties. The Great Depression ended that era of free wheeling prosperity. With jobs hard to find, many were driven into poverty, revealed in this iconic photo by famed female photojournalist Dorothea Lange.

Included in the government agencies and programs established to mitigate growing unemployment, were graphic designers whose talents were put to use creating posters to boost morale and provide encouragement as the Depression years wore on. Their talents would soon be put to other uses.

World War II would offer America's women all the opportunities that the Depression, focused on re-employing men as family breadwinners, did not. Need, not a change in patriarchal thinking, would provide the

Like the Depression, the war was serious business. Whole nations were in the thrall of fanatic leaders, their racist beliefs and nationalist goals making conflict inevitable.

momentum, ultimately overwhelming the resistance of those who still considered a woman's responsibilities to be solely focused on family and home.

Poster art (left, above) proliferated during the Depression years, carrying messages of encouragement to a dispirited nation. World War II would greatly expand the use of posters, with many taking aim at women.

Amelia Earhart

Possessed of talent, courage, and charisma, Amelia Earhart combined assertive self-reliance and femininity in a way that presaged the new opportunities for women made possible by World War II. Earhart emerged as a role model for a new, can-do generation of American women, setting flight records for both distance and speed in the 1920s and '30s. In 1938, seeking to be the first woman to fly solo around the world, she was lost while on the

Earhart (left) is greeted by a member of a far less liberated generation of women, c. 1931. Courageous and self-confident, Earhart was the epitome of the new American woman.

trans-Pacific leg of that flight. Even after her death, she inspired a generation of women aviators, many of whom came to play a role in the war as Women's Air Service Patrol (WASP) pilots.

After America's declaration of war, the appeal to women followed the pattern established in World War I, with posters encouraging patriotism and family, and a focus on the home front.

It was quickly evident, however, that this war was not only a world war in a geographic sense, but was a war that would involve women as well as men. Only with the active participation of women could the war effort succeed. That meant both in civilian and military capacities, with the door wide open to the growing number of women with university degrees and various fields of expertise. By mid-1942, women had become indispensable to the war effort.

Women were encouraged to play an active role in pursuit of victory.

Serving in the Armed Forces

New legislation allowing recruitment of women as active service personnel was needed since existing laws limited service to men, although women had served in an auxiliary status as nurses during and following World War I. The act enabling the Navy to recruit women was approved on July 30, 1942. Within a year, 27,000 WAVES (the acronym for Women Accepted for Volunteer Emergency Service) were in uniform, including a growing number of officers. The WAVES stated objectives (caption below) applied to all military recruiting efforts.

Recruiting posters, circa 1943. The WAVES mission statement read as follows: "To expedite the war effort by releasing... men for duty at sea and their replacement by women in the shore establishment of the Navy, and for other purposes." The results were hundreds of new career opportunities for women.

By the time the first WAVES were being recruited, the Army was already enlisting women. The WAAC (Women's Auxiliary Army Corps) had become operative in May of 1942. In July of '43, the WAAC became the autonomous WAC (Women's Army Corps).

Each of the Armed Forces had a women's auxiliary. Recruitment posters emphasized competence, patriotism, glamour, and wide-ranging career opportunities.

The Coast Guard signed women as SPARS, the name taken from the Coast Guard slogan *Semper Paratus*, Latin for Always Ready, similar to *Semper Fidelis* (Always Faithful), the motto of the United States Marine Corps. The Marines had welcomed women into the Corps starting in

1918, when 300 women enlisted in non-combatant support roles after the United States entered World War I. In WWII, women in the USMC Women's Reserve had the choice of 200 jobs, including positions as code-breaking cryptographers, motion picture camera operators, and as aerial gunnery instructors. Many others had office jobs. By the end of the war, 85% of enlisted personnel assigned to USMC headquarters were women.

"The men treated us very well," a female wartime Marine reminisced. *"They appreciated and respected our commitment."*

Others had a different experience. One WAVE, responding in retrospect to the Navy's 1942 "Release a Man to Fight" campaign, reminisced about a sailor's taunt that summed up a level of resistance to opening enlistment to women.

"Release a man for active duty. Har, har. It takes five of you broads to do what two guys can do!"

There were many who thought that integrating women into the Armed Forces would not succeed, but the realities of total war in an industrial age ultimately proved a compelling reason to buck tradition. In time, most servicemen grew more tolerant and accepting, although another WAVE emphasized how difficult it was to *"… look dignified and ladylike under these circumstances."*

There was similar resistance in the Army establishment, with lengthy hearings that addressed everything from female adaptability to the military's communal lifestyle to the belief that women would merely serve as "companions" to male personnel. Ultimately, existing barracks were modified to house women, while fears of widespread fraternizing by WAC servicewomen proved unfounded.

Tradition had dictated a limited role in the military for women, which continued to mean non-combatant assignments. Newly appointed WAAC commander Oveta Hobby addressed the issue after taking office in 1942. Her staff identified the perception of an American woman as *"…(1) a giddy featherbrain with no interest beyond clothes, cosmetics, and dates; (2) an old battle-ax who loved to boss men around; or (3) a sainted wife and mother, who, out of the kitchen, burned with passion."*

"Waacs (sic) will be neither Amazons rushing

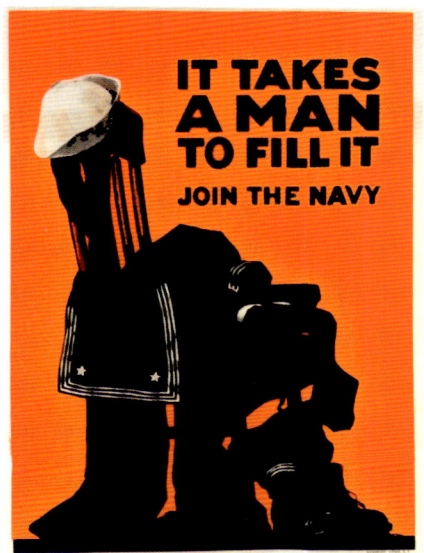

Some in the Armed Forces were opposed to opening the door to women, considering it as damaging to morale and a woman's role maintaining the sanctity of family and home. Others considered proximity ill-advised and impractical. A Navy poster, c.1942, makes the point as some saw it.

to battle, nor fluttering butterflies," responded Hobby soon after taking office as first commander of the WAAC. The Army's women's corps would be *"...a sober, hardworking organization composed of dignified and sensible women."*

Secretary of State Stinson (right) and General Marshall watch as Oveta Hobby is sworn in as first commander of the WAAC in May of 1942. Tens of thousands of women would serve during the war, drawn to military service by recruiting posters.

Two series of recruiting posters focused on expanding the role of women in the WAC during the war years.

Displayed in offices and factories, post offices and train depots, recruiting posters were designed for a quick take, with a straight-forward mix of patriotism, opportunity, glamour, and shared responsibility.

The recruiting effort by the Armed Forces attracted high caliber enlistees who proved dedicated, cooperative, and intelligent partners in the hard-fought pursuit of victory.

On the Home Front

The government's efforts were equally successful on the home front, establishing a sense of partnership between all segments of the population. Women, Blacks, and Americans of all ages and national origins were targeted as partners. There was a role for everyone from grandmothers to newlyweds to the disabled. All were made part of the mainstream effort the war demanded. The recruiting effort significantly increased the number of women in the work force.

"Get a War Job," was the cry, and millions of women did, working in factories and munitions plants, government offices and laboratories, railroads and on farms.

Opposite page: An assembly line of fighter cockpits receives a final go-over by a female work crew (lower left), while a woman mechanic assembles a bomber engine (upper right). As part of the labor force women joined men on picket lines (lower right) when strikes were called.

Loyalty to enlisted servicemen drew women into the work force.

All wars need to be financed, and women were called upon to play their part by purchasing war bonds.

Posters and publicity photos sought to quickly engage, with simple, emotional messages that encouraged a shared sense of national purpose and commitment that included work teams made up of men and women.

Hooray for Hollywood!

The theater arts, with the movies in full bloom, attracted countless women to Broadway and Hollywood. Actresses like Katherine Hepburn, Ingrid Bergman, Lauren Bacall, and Carole Lombard, legendary for their glamour, talent, and intelligence, represented a role model for the American woman as an equal to men, both on screen and off. Using their fame in support of the war effort, they put their lives at risk.

Lombard, an actress and comedienne of academy award caliber, was married to Clark Gable in 1938. Gable, as head of the War Bond effort in the film community, tapped Lombard for a national war bond fund raising tour. She died in a plane crash on Jan. 16, 1942, on her return to Los Angeles. It was a loss that saddened the nation.

Gable and Lombard, c.1940 (left). Betty Grable (below) was the ultimate serviceman's pin-up girl throughout the war years. Top stars like Hedy Lamarr and Lana Turner sold kisses for as much as $50,000 at war bond sales that spoke of the nation's solidarity and commitment. Rita Hayworth (below, right) points to a sign attached to her car. Hollywood's elite joined the nation in recycling materials needed for wartime production.

Marlene Dietrich, circa 1943.

While the majority of OSS women served in administrative roles, some, like actress Marlene Dietrich and entertainer Josephine Baker, served as field operatives. Dietrich, who surrendered her German citizenship in 1937 in opposition to Nazi rule, recorded American songs and anti-Nazi messages that were transmitted from London to the German heartland. She also returned to Europe to entertain American troops and visit the wounded (below). Belgium, Israel and the Netherlands awarded her medals for her work during World War II. America presented her with the Medal of Freedom, its highest civilian honor.

Women also worked with the Office of Strategic Services (OSS) the intelligence-gathering government agency created by executive order of President Franklin Roosevelt in mid-1942. At its peak in 1944, the OSS, forerunner of the Central Intelligence Agency (CIA), had more than 17,000 members, including 4,500 women, more than 26% of the agency's total staff.

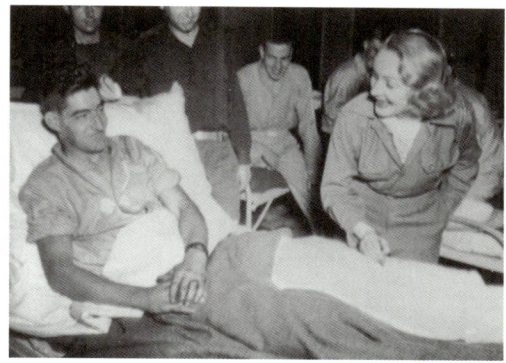

St. Louis-born entertainer Josephine Baker, a superstar in France in the 1920s and '30s, served in the French resistance. Because of her celebrity status, she was able to travel in Europe, relaying information often written on the margins of sheet music. Baker worked with the French Red Cross, becoming involved with the underground resistance starting in 1940, relaying valuable information to the OSS and other security organizations during the war years. Becoming a French citizen in 1937, after the war she was awarded the Medal of the Resistance and the Croix de Guerre, the nation's highest military honor.

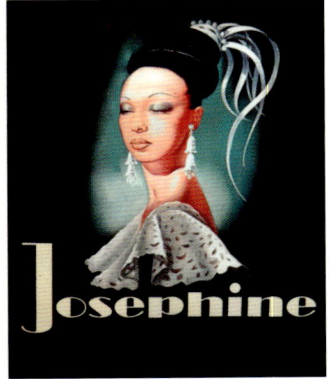

Julia Child, then Julia McWilliams, wanted to join the Navy during World War II but was turned down because she was too tall at six-feet, two-inches. After accepting a job with the OSS soon after the attack on Pearl Harbor, she received the Emblem of Meritorious Civilian Service as head of the registry of the OSS Secretariat in China.

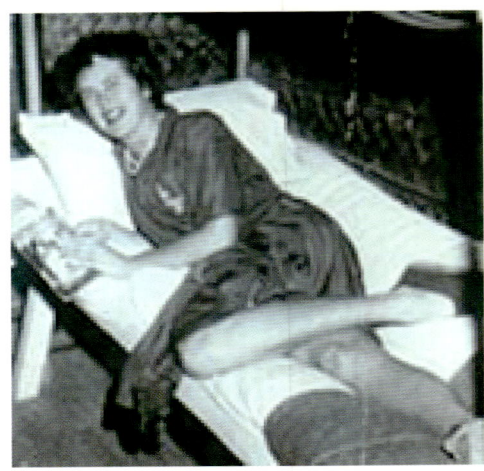

Julia Child, then Julia McWilliams, c. 1944, while serving with the OSS.

Virginia Hall was another legend in the intelligence community. Called the "limping lady of the OSS" because she had a wooden leg, she was the sole civilian female recipient of the Distinguished Service Cross (below), the nation's second-highest award for valor in combat. Turned down by the U.S. Foreign Service because of her gender and limp, she headed to France to join the resistance. Serving as its first female field officer, she engaged in behind-the-lines guerrilla activities. After the war, she became one of the CIA's first female operations officers.

Along with their less famous counterparts, American women played a crucial role in virtually all aspects of OSS activity, working as spies and saboteurs, recruiting agents and cryptographers.

Many women followed their servicemen husbands to stateside postings. My mother, Sue (left), departed Brooklyn in 1943 for Colorado Springs where my father, Milton (center), was an Army sergeant at Camp Carson, then a German POW camp. My aunt (right), came up for a visit from Texas where her husband was stationed. The war broadened the horizons of many American women.

Covering the War... in Words

Long confined to the society page and stories considered of interest to women, the war provided opportunities for women to cover hard news. On the home front, as men were called to fight, increasing numbers of women took over their jobs at the country's newspapers, accounting for more than 50% of the staff by 1943.

The move into reporting from a war front started with Japan's invasion of China in 1937 and continued throughout the war years, with women accounting for 127 of the 1,600 government accredited war correspondents, a dramatic change from WWI, when no women served in that capacity. Despite hostility from some males in the press corps and in the military hierarchy, which sought to restrict women from front line coverage claiming it was too dangerous, correspondents like Martha Gellhorn, who covered the D-Day landings after hiding aboard an in-bound ship. Ruth Cowan and Helen Kirkpatrick gained fame for their wartime reporting. Political columnists Anne McCormick and Dorothy Thompson both received Pulitzer prizes for their coverage.

War correspondents (l to r) Ruth Cowan (Associated Press), Sonia Tomara (New York Herald Tribune), Rosette Hargrove (Newspaper Enterprise Association), Betty Knox (London Evening Standard), Iris Carpenter (Boston Globe), and Erika Mann (Liberty Magazine) gather in Normandy in July 1944, one month after the D-Day invasion. 127 women were ultimately accredited by the military as war correspondents.

...and in Pictures

Having established a world-class reputation as a photographer for *Life* magazine in the 1930s, Margaret Bourke-White would cover the war starting in 1942, when she was the first woman accredited as a war correspondent with the Army Air Corps. Rescued from a torpedoed Navy cruiser en route to North Africa, after a transfer by air was deemed too dangerous, she had to face down the red tape and hostility that women war correspondents and photographers faced.

"There was not a whisper of a double standard," she would later write in her autobiography, *Portrait of Myself*, *"but as though written in invisible ink, it was there for all to read. Male correspondents who applied* [for access to the front lines] *got permission. My requests got nowhere."*

Married to famed novelist Erskine Caldwell, Bourke-White was the first female photographer to cover a live bombing raid. Her powerful images of front line battles raging in Europe and North Africa, included in the book *They Called it Purple Heart Valley*, documented the war, enhancing her reputation as one of the 20th century's greatest photojournalists.

Photographer Lee Miller, whose free-spirited lifestyle and surrealist work defined her as an avant-garde celebrity in the 1920s and '30s, gained additional

Burke-White atop the Chrysler Building, c. 1930. Her photo of liberated prisoners at the Buchenwald concentration camp.

fame shooting for Condé Nast publications during World War II, providing a link between the worlds of war and fashion. In Paris, when it was liberated from Nazi control, Miller documented Parisian fashion for *Vogue* before heading off to provide front line coverage of the Allied capture of Strasbourg and the nightmarish reality of the Nazi concentration camps at Dachau and Buchenwald. Talented photographer Dickey Chapelle made her way to Japan to cover the finale of the war in the Pacific.

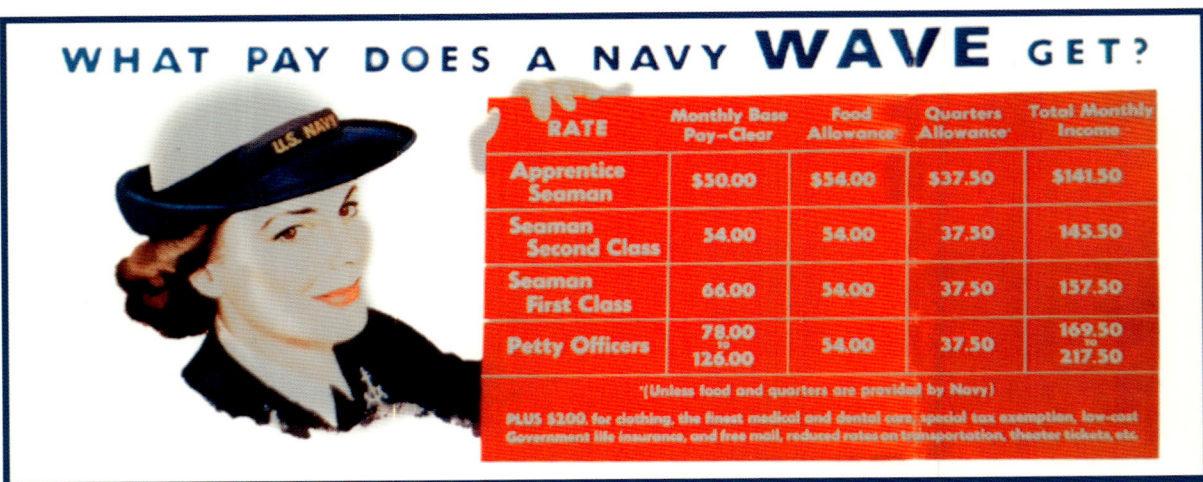

WHAT PAY DOES A NAVY WAVE GET?

RATE	Monthly Base Pay – Clear	Food Allowance*	Quarters Allowance*	Total Monthly Income
Apprentice Seaman	$50.00	$54.00	$37.50	$141.50
Seaman Second Class	54.00	54.00	37.50	145.50
Seaman First Class	66.00	54.00	37.50	157.50
Petty Officers	78.00 to 126.00	54.00	37.50	169.50 to 217.50

*(Unless food and quarters are provided by Navy)

PLUS $200. for clothing, the finest medical and dental care, special tax exemption, low-cost Government life insurance, and free mail, reduced rates on transportation, theater tickets, etc.

Women were lured into military service with pay and benefits comparable to what was offered to men. Women would find true equality in the workplace an elusive goal. On the home front, women were paid about one-third less than men for comparable work: a male factory worker earned an average $55.00 per week, while for woman the average was $31.00. After the war years, unions would make "equal pay for equal work" a contract goal. Today, women continue to receive only about 75% of the pay offered men for similar work.

Serving as Volunteers

Millions of women also served in volunteer organizations like the American Red Cross, which was already involved in preparedness projects initiated by the government when war was declared on December 8, 1941. The Red Cross quickly mobilized, fulfilling its congressionally chartered mission to *"…furnish volunteer aid to the sick and wounded of armies in time of war"* and to *"…act in matters of voluntary relief and in accord with the military and naval authorities as medium of communication between the people of the United States of America and their Army and Navy."*

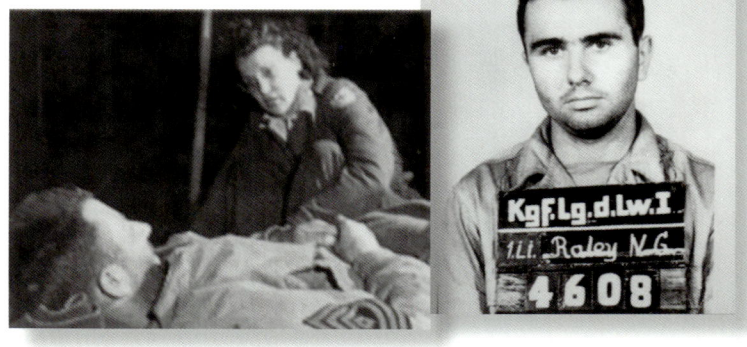

Following the D-Day landings along France's Normandy coast on June 6, 1944, men and women with the American Red Cross helped establish "evacuation hospitals" behind the front lines, moving forward as the Allied invasion advanced, working in the shadow of battlefield violence. The American Red Cross also served the 1.4 million Allied prisoners of war, like POW Nathaniel Raley (above right). 13,500 volunteers, mostly women, prepared 27 million packages for Allied POWs.

During World War I, Red Cross nurses served side-by-side with military nurses. In WWII, the military role of the American Red Cross was limited to recruiting nurses for the rapidly expanding Army and Navy Nursing Corps. An estimated 153,000 nurses, the majority women, held 'active' status on Red Cross rolls, with 71,000 serving in the military. By 1944-45, there were also 110,000 Red Cross-trained, nurses' aides serving nationwide.

In January 1941 the U.S. military asked the American Red Cross to organize a Blood Donor Service to meet the anticipated needs of America's Armed Forces should war become a reality. At its peak, the program had a paid staff of 2,285 doctors, nurses, and technicians, and a largely female work force of 39,000. In addition, millions of female volunteers provided numerous services to the military and on the home front.

During the war years the American Red Cross operated 35 donor centers and 63 mobile units, collecting 13.4 million life-saving pints of blood from more than 6.5 million donors.

The United Service Organization (USO) provided women with yet another opportunity to serve. The USO was formed in mid-1941 at the request of President Roosevelt in response to the growing likelihood of war and the necessary expansion of the American military. It was an all-volunteer civilian organization created to provide links between the home front and the battlefront, offering *"...compassion and reassurance from the ordinary citizen"* to the

On the home front, the Red Cross provided classes in first aid, civil defense, and proper nutrition, served in hospitals, produced emergency supplies for war victims, collected scrap for recycling, and helped with Victory Gardens. The Red Cross also operated canteens at military installations, train stations, ports of embarkation, and military airfields, with mobile canteens serving military personnel overseas.

Volunteers dance with servicemen at a USO club.

men defending the country. By war's end, 1.5 million volunteers, the majority women and often the wives and daughters of servicemen, had served with the USO. The more than 3,000 USO clubs in virtually every part of the country and overseas had hosted an astonishing 428,521 performances and events.

Jane Hammond volunteered at military hospitals in New York City, singing for wounded soldiers with the American Theater Wing, visiting troops brought stateside from the front lines.

"I volunteered for three years, going to the hospitals after work three days a week, strolling through the wards singing to these wounded boys. We were the first girls they saw. They were all babies, just 17 or 18. I was 19, so they were my peers. They appreciated it so. I felt we owed it to them: That was my contribution."

More than 7,000 entertainers participated in USO shows, including "A" list stars like the Andrews Sisters (left), songstress Jane Froman, critically injured when her plane crashed returning from USO shows in Europe, and Dinah Shore. Shore sings for American troops in France in August 1944 (above), one of a number of front line shows she headlined in for the USO. She also aired more than 300 shows that were broadcast to troops on the Armed Forces Radio Network. She was honored for her efforts with a USO Medallion.

In keeping with its home front efforts, the government promoted a symbol of the new American woman, who debuted in 1942 in a poster released by the Westinghouse Corporation to boost factory morale. "We Can Do It!", she proclaimed confidently, determined and beautiful, her arm extended in a muscular fist, sleeves rolled up on her workday blues.

Artist Norman Rockwell would create an equally iconic image of the new working women. His 'Rosie the Riveter' was a potent symbol, an unusual mix of patriotism and working class glamour that resonated with the public and succeeded in making working outside the home, once widely condemned, socially acceptable.

Rosie the Riveter, part glamour, part brawn, as conceived by artist Norman Rockwell for the May 29, 1943 cover of the Saturday Evening Post. Sandwich in hand, she is dressed in workplace blues with wartime badges on her blouse and a halo overhead. Armed with a riveting gun, her feet rest on a copy of Mein Kampf. The war had now been raging for 18-months and the American woman was playing an increasingly crucial role in the war effort. There were, indeed, thousands of real Rosie's…women who quickly mastered factory jobs and assured a steady flow of vital supplies and munitions for the war.

Words and music glorify the new American women. While Rosie the Riveter's origin is a matter of some dispute, she became a wartime icon.

Participation of women in the nation's economy was the name of the game, and the government encouraged women to do anything that might help in the war effort.

Poster to boost morale, 1942.

That not only meant jobs in factories and offices, but also by planting Victory Gardens to provide food for home use, thus freeing supplies for the military, helping with the summer harvest, and working at non-traditional occupations. A range of government agencies, like the U.S. Crop Corps and the U.S. Employment Service, promoted women's participation in the war effort.

Women loggers at work in Washington State (below), c. 1943. From office to factory to farm, women were encouraged to use skills familiar and newly learned in support of the war effort.

For some men and women freedom meant testing the limits. The result was growing concern over the spread of sexually transmitted diseases, particularly within the military, where the consequences were potentially disastrous to the war effort. As a result, the government sponsored poster campaigns that focused on awareness and protection, part of a program on health awareness that aimed at both men and women.

On the national scene, Eleanor Roosevelt proved an impressive role model, widely respected for her sharp intellect, humanistic values, and her high-profile role as First Lady. Roosevelt traveled widely on behalf of the war effort, visiting troops in the field and war plants at home, spearheading fund raising efforts, working with the Red

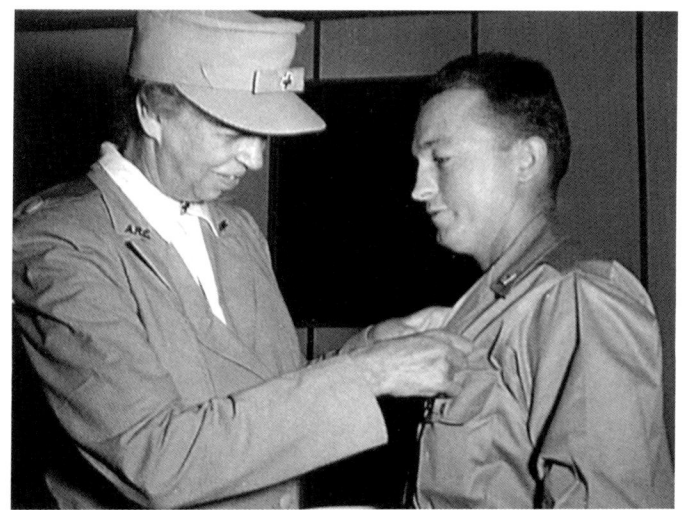

Like many American women, First Lady Eleanor Roosevelt (left) played multiple roles during World War II. Her Red Cross cap identifies her strong links to that organization as she pins a Purple Heart on a soldier while visiting New Caledonia, in the western Pacific, in 1943.

Cross, and in confidence-building speaking tours. Intelligent, independent, self-confident, and accomplished, a woman of high integrity, she set an example that has inspired many in the decades-long push for equality that has followed.

For the 13 years of the Depression and throughout the war years that marked her husband's presidency, she provided a sense of stability, confidence, and hope. If the war had changed women's status, Eleanor Roosevelt was proof of the potential that women were now free to pursue.

The political landscape, however, remained a male preserve, with women fewer than 1% of the total membership of the combined houses of Congress. Best known of that select group was Clare Boothe Luce, who served as a Republican from Connecticut in the House of Representatives, and later as Ambassador to Italy and Brazil. Women remain underrepresented in the halls of Congress, although key leadership roles for women have become a hallmark of contemporary America.

The demands of the war effort provided a new social and economic paradigm for the postwar era, although not without facing some very real challenges en route. The first was confronted when the war came to an end in 1945 and the Armed Forces released millions of men from active service.

VJ Day (Victory over Japan) marked Japan's surrender on August 14th, 1945. The formal surrender papers were signed on the USS Missouri on September 2.

Jubilation was widespread following VJ Day. It soon became obvious, however, that there was a price to be paid for peace, with millions of returning servicemen meaning fewer jobs for women.

The government now found itself responsible for reintegrating those who had served in the military into a still nascent civilian economy, facilitating their return to civilian life with educational and vocational programs.

Not surprisingly, the government and industry had looked at women as a temporary solution to an immediate need. In many factories, retooling from war production to consumer goods, women were fired and encouraged to return home, leaving the jobs for returning servicemen.

In the military, men and women would find themselves decommissioned as the Armed Forces dramatically downsized. Of the 18,460 women in the Marine Corps at the end of the war, for example, all but 1,000 were released.

Little was made of women's wartime contributions. *"When I was a schoolgirl, right after the war ended,"* said Julia Goetz thinking back 65 years, *"when we studied the war, there was almost nothing mentioned about the important role women played in the war effort."*

The war, however, had changed the social and economic status of women. For single women and others grown used to a paycheck and a life outside the home, there was no turning back, particularly as the economy expanded in the 1950s and '60s and women once again found the door opening to new opportunities.

As it turned out, as the postwar economy boomed, it created jobs for both returning servicemen as well as millions of women. Decade-by-decade, there were increases in the number of women in the workplace.

For American women, World War II proved a world-changing, life-changing event, an extension of efforts begun nearly a century earlier by Susan B. Anthony and other Suffragettes. It also served as a prelude to the feminist movement that followed.

The true scope of the transformation that has taken place since World War II is evident in statistics compiled in the Shriver Report and in a survey by the Rockefeller Foundation and *Time* detailed in a cover story dated October 26, 2009. It is indeed a new America that emerges from these statistics, an America in which women are a full half of the work force, and families with dual breadwinners now the norm.

Another barrier broken

Army veteran becomes first woman to command school for drill sergeants

BY SUSANNE M. SCHAFER
Associated Press

FORT JACKSON, S.C. — Command Sgt. Maj. Teresa King can dress down a burly, battle-hardened sergeant in seconds with a sharp phrase and a withering look, then turn around and tell trainee soldiers to be sure they get seven hours of sleep.

As the first woman to take charge of the Army's school for its order-barking drill sergeants, the 28-year military veteran and sharecropper's daughter said she's used to breaking down barriers in military roles normally reserved for men.

"It's so easy because I love it," said King, a single, 48-year-old North Carolina native. "I have a family in the Army. It is my family."

The stern discipline dispensed by her late father to his 12 children set her on a path of taking responsibility for herself and her siblings early on, King said during a recent interview on the Army's training base next to Columbia, S.C.

She learned to "give a hard day's work for whatever I earned and take no short cuts," said King, who enjoys passing her values to young soldiers and watching them grow into senior officers and enlisted men and women.

Lt. Col. Dave Wood, King's battalion commander, said she was chosen for her approach to "the business of taking civilians and making them into soldiers."

Gone are the days of two decades ago, Wood said, when his drill sergeant made him clean wax off a floor with a razor blade or run around the barracks loaded down with a full duffel bag.

"She's got this unique way of dealing with soldiers where she

SEE LEADER, A22

Living and Fighting Alongside Men, and Fitting In

From Page A1

Iraq over the next year.

"We've needed — needed — the contributions of both our men and women," said Brig. Gen. Mary A. Legere, the director of intelligence for the American war effort here and the other highest ranking woman in Iraq.

The military, of course, is not gender blind, especially in a war zone.

Sexual harassment in a still-predominantly male institution remains a problem. So does sexual assault. Both are underreported, soldiers and officers here say, because the rigidity of the military chain of command can make any... described the experience as isolating.

"I always felt like the plague," she said at Warhorse, on her second tour in Iraq, where she handles communications for the commander of the First Stryker Brigade of the 25th Infantry Division.

As the United States military settled into more permanent bases, many initial difficulties abated, as the Army gradually adapted to the new reality of waging war with a mixed force. So have the soldiers themselves.

Women have sought acceptance in a still-predominantly male environment not by emphasizing their sex but rather...

Women do become pregnant — a condition that, intentional or not, in or out of wedlock, requires the woman to be flown out within two weeks, causing personnel disruptions in individual units.

The Army and Marine Corps declined to say exactly how many women left Iraq and Afghanistan as a result of pregnancies, but it appears to be relatively rare and has had little effect on overall readiness, commanders say. At Warhorse, the First Stryker Brigade, which has thousands of soldiers, has sent only three women home because of...

Like many commanders who have served in Iraq or Afghanistan, he said that women have ended the debate over their role by their performance.

"I've relieved males from command," he said. "I've never relieved a female commander in two and a half years as commander."

The nature of the war has also done much to change the debate over combat roles. Any trip off the heavily secured bases now effectively invites contact with the enemy.

Many women have also been pulled off their regular jobs and trained to...

Articles in this series explore how the wars in Iraq and Afghanistan have profoundly redefined the role of women in the military.

ONLINE: THE BATTLEFIELD REMADE
Hear women serving as soldiers and commanders reflect on their combat experiences at
nytimes.com/world
● A video report from Forward

Three headlines dated September and October 2009 reveal the on-going process of fully integrating women into America's Armed Forces. It has taken more than 65 years for full service equality to become accepted policy. It is a transformation that has also been underway in the civilian workplace, with women now a full half of the American work force, with high-profile roles as executives, scientists, lawyers, educators, artists, public officials, entertainers and entrepreneurs. While some barriers remain, with pay differentials still the norm, the pattern of accomplishment established during World War II has continued during the largely prosperous decades that have followed. It's been an uphill fight, a call for equity that has meant changing social perceptions, transforming American society in the process.

The Honolulu Advertiser

Women to serve on subs

Navy's integration plan could have first female officers on board by 2011

BY WILLIAM COLE
Advertiser Military Writer

The Navy is preparing to notify Congress of a change that would put women on some submarines for the first time — but not initially on the attack submarines that are based at Pearl Harbor.

The first female accessions into the submarine force could come as early as 2010, the Navy said. They would begin training for submarine duty, consisting of nuclear power school, prototype training and the submarine officer basic course.

Upon completion of the coursework, the first female officers could report to submarines in 2011.

"This is something (Chief of Naval Operations Adm. Gary Roughead) and I have been working on since I came into office," Secretary of the Navy Ray Mabus said in a directive issued on the change. "We are moving out aggressively on this. I believe women should have every opportunity to serve at sea, and that includes aboard submarines."

The sea service said it envisions initially assigning female officers to larger ballistic missile and guided missile submarines because they have more available space for officer accommodations, would require less modification and would allow the Navy to move more quickly.

"Our efforts there will inform our...

SEE WOMEN, A2

It's a wide-ranging transformation, with women now serving on the Supreme Court, in the Cabinet, and in Congress, with a fast-growing number of women lawyers, doctors, professors, university presidents, news correspondents, corporate CEOs, and Nobel laureates revealing the many ways women have become integrated into the work force. Even that bastion of male exclusivity, the Federal Bureau of Investigation, has been impacted, with 2,396 women on the FBI's payroll in 2009, compared to none in the 1972.

> THE NEW YORK TIMES **BUSINESS** WEDNESDAY, NOVEMBER 11, 2009
>
> ## Survey Finds Deep Shift In the Makeup of Unions
>
> ### Fewer Factory Workers and More Women
>
> By STEVEN GREENHOUSE
>
> A study has found that just one in 10 union members is in manufacturing, while women account for more than 45 percent of the unionized work force.
>
> The study, by the Center for
>
> ization efforts in the private sector.
>
> The study found that white men represent just 38 percent of all union members and that women will come to represent more than half of all union members during the next decade.

University statistics reveal a similar leveling of the playing field, with women now out-numbering men on the nation's college campuses 57 to 43, and matching men in the number pursuing doctoral, medical and legal degrees.

More independence has had other demographic consequences, with increasingly self-reliant women marrying later (at 26 vs. 21 in 1972), with the number of never-married women doubling, from 5% in 1972 to 10% today. The study also revealed that 39% of today's children are born outside of marriage, that 23% of American children are now raised in mother-only families, and that women are the primary breadwinner in nearly 40% of families.

Yet inequities remain, with women receiving only 77 cents for every dollar earned by men for comparable work, a raised "glass ceiling" still intact, and full gender equality still an elusive goal.

Necessity, created by the war opened a door, and reality for the American woman would never be quite the same. In the millions of women who answered the call, we glimpse a future that they would help make possible for their children, grandchildren, and the generations that follow.

Women now represent 45% of union membership in the U.S.(left).
A poster (right), circa 1942, praises the wartime effort of America's working women.

A poster, c. 1942, acknowledges the important role women played in the war effort.

© Allan Seiden/Legacy Archive Press, Hon., Hawaii, 2017

Letter Postage Required

A comic look at the changing role of the
American woman during WWII.

© Allan Seiden/Legacy Archive Press, Hon., Hawaii, 2017

Letter
Postage
Required

All the Armed Forces actively recruited women throughout the war years. More than 100,000 ultimately served.

© Allan Seiden/Legacy Archive Press, Hon., Hawaii, 2017

Letter Postage Required